Work Readiness™

great lifelong learning skills

jeanne nagle

ROSEN
PUBLISHING®

New York

*Special thanks to Matt and Jared for all their
technical assistance during the writing of this book*

Published in 2008 by The Rosen Publishing Group, Inc.
29 East 21st Street, New York, NY 10010

Library of Congress Cataloging-in-Publication Data

Nagle, Jeanne.
Great lifelong learning skills / Jeanne Nagle.
    p. cm.—(Work readiness)
Includes bibliographical references and index.
ISBN-13: 978-1-4042-1424-8 (library binding)
1. Continuing education. 2. Learning. 3. Teenagers—Life skills
guides. I. Title.
LC5215.N243 2008
374—dc22

                                                    2007032650

Manufactured in the United States of America

contents

Wouldn't it be great if you could wish for something to happen and then, without doing anything, your dream would come true? For instance, perhaps you decide it would be great to have a certain job, even though you don't know much about the field and you have no experience doing the tasks that are required for this job. You apply for the position anyway, and the company hires you on the spot.

Unfortunately, things don't usually work out that way. To find, get, and keep a job that you like and that pays well, it helps to have a plan to guide your way. You need to prepare yourself by determining your goals for lifelong learning, especially as they relate to your job and your future work.

Being willing and able to continue learning, every day in a thousand different ways, is the best preparation you can have for lifelong learning. The reasons are simple. Every bit of knowledge and every skill you gain makes you look good to employers. They want to hire people who are smart and flexible, and they give bonuses and promote those who can keep up to date on the latest and best ways to perform a job. Employees who prove they are open to new ideas and skills through a commitment to lifelong learning are admired and sought after in the workplace.

The most important point about learning is that anyone, just about anywhere, can do it. No matter how educated you are, how many work-related skills you may already have, or how much you think you can afford, there is a way for you to continue to learn.

There is a practical side to the benefits of lifelong learning as well. Job demands change all the time. Technology (such as computer software) and procedures, or ways of performing job tasks, are constantly being updated or improved to help employees do their jobs faster and better. If you don't learn a company's frequently changing procedures and goals, you may find yourself out of a job.

Still, if you're only learning so that you can keep your job, you're missing out on something great. When you're open to new experiences, the whole world becomes much more interesting. And you become a lot more appealing to the people who can hire you.

chapter one

TAKE RESPONSIBILITY FOR LEARNING

When you're younger, it seems as if everybody has something to say about whether or not you get an education. When you're about four or five years old, your parents send you to school or, in some families, start your homeschooling. They make sure you attend classes, do your homework, and get good grades. If you skip school, you get in trouble with your parents, the school's principal, and your teachers. In the United States and Canada, depending on the law in each state or province, you have to attend high school until you graduate or are between the ages of sixteen and eighteen. So, if you are absent for too long without a good reason, which is called being truant, even the police might become involved. Many people spend lots of time making sure that you learn.

As you get older, though, the situation changes. Once you've reached a certain age or graduated from high school, nobody forces you to go to school. No one makes a point of exposing you to new and interesting facts. After a while, you're pretty much on your own when it comes to learning.

Taking responsibility for learning goes beyond participating in the classroom. It means finding ways to make learning a lifelong habit.

Taking responsibility for what you learn is a job that lasts a lifetime. Successful people are constantly learning. The more you learn, the more options you have. This is especially true when it comes to finding and keeping a good job. When you think about where you will work and what kind of work you'd like to do, the last thing you want is to limit yourself.

Luckily, taking charge of your education to obtain employment doesn't have to be a problem. All it takes is preparation. Think about your situation, decide what the best methods are for you to learn, and establish job-related goals based on what you discover about yourself. Then investigate and take advantage of learning opportunities that will help you achieve those goals.

Take Stock

Take a close look at who you are, who you'd like to become, and what you need to bridge the gap between those two places in your life. This process is called taking stock because it's similar to making an inventory. Just as a shop owner surveys or sees what stock items are available at his or her store and what's missing from the shelves, you can do likewise with your skills.

The first step is to consider what you already are capable of doing. Maybe you can draw, fix machines, solve complex math problems, bake amazing desserts, organize events, or talk to people and make them feel better—anything you think you're good at doing or those abilities other people have mentioned to you that you do well. These can be either traits or talents that you've come by naturally or skills you have learned and

Even skills you might think have nothing to do with work, such as baking, can be useful in your job search.

mastered. They can be abilities you just learned recently or picked up a while ago.

Next, figure out if and how these skills might be useful at work. Sometimes, you have to look a little deeper to see the full worth of your abilities. For instance, you wouldn't expect that baking desserts would be a useful skill on the job—unless you wanted to be a baker. However, there are certain skills involved in cooking and baking that translate into job pluses, such as the ability to follow directions. You can find learning value in so many tasks you already know how to do.

Strengths and Weaknesses

When you take stock, you'll discover that you have both strengths and weakness when it comes to learning. Your strengths are the skills you do well, tasks that you feel are easy to do and that you enjoy doing.

Putting your strengths and weaknesses down on paper gives you a clearer picture of where you stand and what areas need work.

Then there are your weaknesses. These are areas that need improvement—shortcomings that you can amend through learning. In terms of getting and keeping a good job, an example of a weakness would be when you don't have the proper skills for a particular type of work, or you have the skills but you need to build on them.

Know Your Learning Style

Everyone typically has a preferred learning style. This is a specific way in which you seem to be more willing and able to take in, understand, and remember information. Experts have narrowed down learning styles based on three of the five senses: seeing, hearing, and touch.

1. Visual learners might learn by listening to a teacher presenting a lecture in class, but the information really sinks in when they have something visual to study that goes with the discussion. When visuals are not available, they try to pick up extra clues about what's being said by watching the speaker's face and body language. Pictures, diagrams, video, or even notes that they take during class help them understand and retain, or keep in mind, what they have learned.

2. Auditory learners gain knowledge best by listening. During a demonstration, they get more out of what the presenter is saying than by what he or she is showing them. Auditory learners like to take part in discussions because using words is a strength for them. Tape-recording a lecture and playing it back, rather than taking notes, may be a better way for them to study.

3. Tactile learners prefer to be taught by doing. They take a hands-on approach when it comes to investigating new tasks. Sitting in a classroom and either listening or reading may be difficult for them. They like to be on the move, exploring how things work firsthand. Building a model and making it work would teach them more about a subject or concept than reading about it or hearing someone explain how something is supposed to work.

This manager is using visual (showing plans), auditory (speaking with the worker), and tactile (preparing to build something together) learning techniques. Using multiple approaches can help you improve learning.

One of these styles might be preferred by you more than the others. If so, you'll want to find ways to learn new job skills that involve that style. For instance, if you are an auditory learner, you would do well going to a seminar and hearing speakers talk about their areas of expertise. Likewise, if you're a tactile learner, you'd be better off in a class where students are involved in hands-on learning. However, you may also feel pretty comfortable learning in all these ways or in some combination of the three. Combinations are good because they give you even more chances to learn.

Set Goals

Once you have figured out where there's room for improvement in your learning, set learning goals. Setting goals lets you be specific about what you want to accomplish. Goals break down large tasks such as lifelong learning into smaller chunks that are easier to complete.

One effective way to set goals is to make a list of the weaknesses you want to focus on and then, alongside each example, list the actions you can take to overcome these weaknesses. What you write in the second column will be your goals.

Be honest with yourself when setting goals and make sure that what you hope to learn is possible, given your situation. Take into account where you live, what resources are available, any other responsibilities you have, and what your financial situation is, among other issues. Also, give yourself time to reach each goal. Don't rush yourself, and don't get overly frustrated if it takes a while to get there.

Explore Opportunities to Learn About Work

There are lots of opportunities to become educated. One option is going to a four-year or two-year (junior) college. You will take classes in a major, which is a group of courses that cover a subject area from all sorts of angles. You will also strengthen your communication skills in college, as well as your ability to socialize and work with others.

College is not the right choice for everyone, however. With that in mind, there are a few other ways to learn work skills.

Career and Technical Education

Also known as trade school or vocational training, career and technical education lets you focus your studies on a specific job field. The most common subject areas covered by career and technical education are business and skilled trades, like automotive technology, nursing, dental and medical technology, culinary arts (cooking), marketing, construction, and life skills.

Career and technical education classes are taught in public schools, in schools specially designed to offer career training, or through community programs at various locations in your city or town. Anyone from high school students to adults can participate in career and technical education programs. Experts at the U.S. Office of Educational Research and Improvement estimate that eleven million people in the United States take advantage of this kind of learning, so you know you'll

Taking classes that teach you a trade, such as being a computer technician, is a great alternative, or addition, to a two- or four-year college experience.

be in good company if you decide to follow this path. Along with classes, this type of education gives you firsthand work experience through apprenticeships and internships.

Apprenticeships and Internships

An apprenticeship is one of the oldest forms of training in the world. As an apprentice, you learn a craft or trade, such as jewelry making or plumbing, by actually doing the work while being coached by an expert in the field. You move through an apprenticeship at a gradual pace, proving you can perform at one level before moving on to the next. The pay isn't much in the beginning, but your salary tends to go up as you get better at your work. Instead of being awarded a diploma, you receive a certificate at the end of your training that shows employers and customers that you are capable of doing the job. Apprenticeships can be a particularly good option if you are a tactile or hands-on learner.

Internships are similar in that you learn by doing, except you're trained to perform tasks more than to specifically create or fix things. If they get paid at all, interns receive a stipend—a small sum of money they get throughout their time at work. As an intern, you might get some kind of certificate when you finish your training. More likely, the person who has been your boss will write you a letter of recommendation, which tells future employers that you are a good worker and you did your job well. In some cases, interns who perform very well are asked to stay on at a company or organization and become permanent, paid employees.

Job Corps

The purpose of America's federally funded Job Corps program is to help you get an entry-level job in the field of your choice. Students who are between the ages of sixteen and twenty-four, are U.S. citizens, and are from low-income households may learn a trade, earn a high school diploma, or get a General Educational Development (GED) certificate. In addition to career training, you'll also take classes in academic subjects and learn skills that will make you more attractive to employers. After you finish training, you'll also get help in finding a job.

Joining the program is free, and students receive housing, meals, medical care, and a biweekly allowance while they participate. Job Corps centers are located across the United States.

Experience

Learning doesn't happen only in formal settings such as school or other structured programs. You can get a certain amount of education through the activities you do every day or have done in the past. For example, if you've ever babysat, you learned how to take care of children and help run a household. This may not qualify you to run a day care center, but it can be a step in that direction.

Experience teaches you something, and the more experience you have, the more you learn. In fact, many colleges give course credit for certain types of life and work experience, and employers are always looking for people who have experience.

Programs such as the U.S. Job Corps provide classes on a variety of academic subjects (including basic reading and math) and social skills, in addition to career training courses.

Be Willing to Learn

Perhaps the most significant part of taking responsibility for learning involves your attitude. You have to be willing to learn. You should be curious, as well as open to new ideas and ways of doing things. You should look for ways to improve and not wait for opportunities to come to you.

Above all else, you must take learning seriously. You should really put your mind to it. Without that commitment, little else that you do will make a difference.

chapter two

LEARN THROUGH RESEARCH

Wherever you work, and no matter what kind of job you have, you need to be able to think and work independently. First, other people can't tell you every-thing there is to know about your job, and they certainly can't predict how you will respond in certain situations. Second, there will be times when problems occur that haven't happened before, and you'll need to deal with them as they happen. Consequently, you will have to find some things out for yourself. To do this, you'll need to conduct research.

How to Conduct Research

Research is an organized way to gather information. You've already done research, for example, when you read books and reported on them for school, or when you conducted experiments in science class. In these instances, you started with a question that you either asked yourself or that your teacher asked you: "What is this book about?" "What happens when I mix these chemicals?" Then you began your investigation by

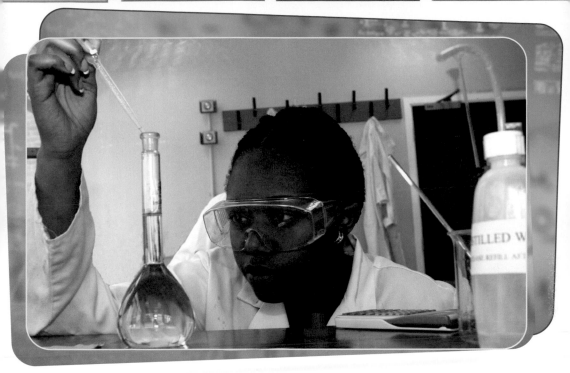

Anytime you ask questions, gather data, test theories, and come to a conclusion, you are conducting research. Science experiments are an example of research.

reading the book or combining the chemicals. You made notes and recorded the information in some way, explaining to yourself what happened, what you learned, and what you thought about the experience. Then you put all your notes and observations together to come to a conclusion, which is an answer to your original question. That's research.

There's a lot of information out there on just about any subject you can name. Unless you're pretty certain about what it is you're researching, you could wind up being confused or find yourself with a lot of useless

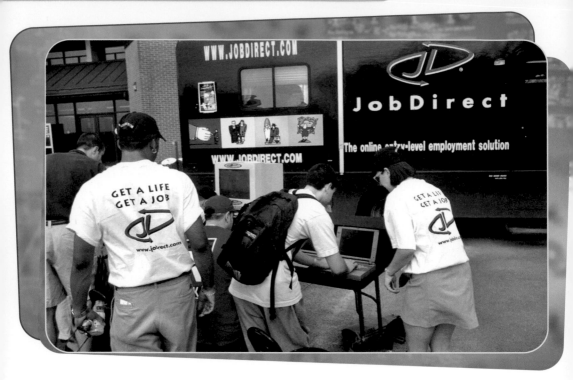

You should take advantage of job search resources wherever and whenever you can. Many Web sites are available to help you find work.

facts. The more specific your question or topic is, the easier and faster it is to conduct the respective research.

Use Many Sources

Different sources will give you different viewpoints on a subject, even if they cover the same basic material. Checking lots of diverse places also helps you feel confident that what you're discovering about a subject is the truth. Any one source can make a claim that may be false or have an error. If you see a fact or a statistic repeated by several sources, that doesn't mean you can be 100 percent sure that it's true. Still, chances are better that the information is accurate when you see the same information given in more than one place.

Also, each type of source gives you an opportunity to stretch various skills. Electronic sources such as the Internet give you a chance to practice your computer and Web search abilities. During interviews, you can obtain experience with interpersonal (dealing with other people), communication, and listening skills, which you'll need while working at any job.

Print and electronic media and informational interviews are some sources that will help you with your work research.

Print and Electronic Media

The word "media" refers to the ways in which information is collected and presented to the public. Books, news-papers, and magazines are examples of print media. Television, radio, video and audio recordings, and Internet Web sites (see also chapter 3) are electronic media.

You can check out different jobs by reading career books and brochures that might be available in your school's guidance office, the school or public library, and your community's employment office. These sources may also have videotapes and audio recordings that cover specific careers or general employment tips. In addition, read newspaper and magazine articles or watch television news shows that provide information on the fields you're interested in or that profile someone who has the same job that you want.

10 Great Questions to Ask

1. How did you get started in this field?

2. What level of education did you have when you started this job?

3. How would you describe an average day at work?

4. What are your most and least favorite aspects of this job?

5. What kind of on-the-job training have you received since you've been here?

6. How heavy is competition for a position similar to yours?

7. If you were in hiring, what would your reaction to my resume be?

8. What steps would you recommend I take next to get a job in this field?

9. Are there any organizations I can join or books I can read that might teach me more about this field?

10. Do you know of anyone else I could speak with about this type of career?

Interviews and Surveys

If you don't know about a certain field or job, ask about it. This is one of the simplest forms of research. Talk to people who work in a field that interests you. For instance, you can attend a career fair at your school and have a conversation with the employers who are working at the booths there. Explain that you're interested in their line of work and that you'd like to find out more about their job in general and their company in particular.

Another way to conduct research is to contact a company that is involved in the kind of work you'd like to do and ask if you could conduct an informational interview. Such an interview will enable you to find out what a job specifically involves by asking questions of someone who is actually performing that type of work, one-on-one in a professional setting.

Experiments

An experiment is when you test a theory to find out if what you think is going to happen actually does happen. The circumstance you think is going to happen is called a hypothesis. If the experiment doesn't go as you had planned, you'll have to figure out why the outcome was different from what you had expected.

So, when it comes to finding a job, how do you experiment? You try out different occupations. Sampling jobs is a great way to find out if you would like to make a line of work your career. The following are a few ways to try out an occupation:

- **Community programs.** Organizations such as the YMCA offer classes centered on occupations and career-related hobbies.
- **Cooperative education programs.** These programs provide you with classes for half a day and with work outside the classroom for the rest of the day.
- **Entrepreneurship.** This involves your starting and managing your own business.
- **Part-time and temporary jobs.** Even if you don't hold the exact job you want, working part-time or on a temporary basis can give you an insider's view of a particular career field.
- **Clubs.** Joining a club that focuses on your chosen career gives you contacts with people who have similar interests and keeps you up-to-date on the latest trends in the field, as well as being a positive addition to your resume.
- **Shadowing.** This activity involves following and observing someone on the job for a day or two.
- **Specialized summer camps/schools.** These environments enable you to take classes focused on your career interests over summer vacation.
- **Volunteer.** Giving an organization or group a little of your time will enable you to gain some practical hands-on experience.

Your Experiences

Review the work you have performed in the past. It can be either paid work for a commercial employer (for example, in a store or office), self-employment (mowing lawns, babysitting), or even volunteer work. Each of

Tips on Informational Interviews

Prepare a list of questions before you conduct your interview. Try to ask questions that will allow the other person to explain how he or she thinks and feels about the subject, not just the plain facts. Ask follow-up questions if you're not clear about the answer you've been given, or if you feel you need more information.

There's a trick reporters use that might help you. Ask questions in a way that makes it impossible for the person you're interviewing to answer with a simple "yes" or "no." For example, if a reporter interviews someone who has just been robbed, he or she wouldn't ask, "Were you frightened?" The better question would be, "What were you feeling when the thief demanded your wallet?" Carefully word your questions and you'll get a lot of useful information in return.

When you receive a response, listen carefully. Also, don't be surprised if the answers you get to your questions lead you to ask additional questions. Something a person says may lead you down a path that you never even thought of previously, and following that path might teach you a lot.

Research jobs for which you might be interested in applying: Conduct informational interviews to help you research these jobs.

chapter three
USE INFORMATION AND COMMUNICATIONS TECHNOLOGY

Technology plays a major role in your everyday life. Computers are used in offices, stores, libraries, and homes around the world. Computer technology also runs many items you've come to rely on, from cars to televisions and appliances such as microwave ovens. The way you spend your free time can also depend on technology—for example, taking vacation photos with a digital camera or spending an afternoon playing video games. In addition, many people would be lost without their cell phones.

As for the workplace, it would be hard to find a job that doesn't require the use of some form of communications or information technology in the daily routine. Finding and getting a job is a lot easier when you use technological resources such as a computer and the Internet. Therefore, you should learn about the technology and equipment you might encounter at work.

Computers

Workers around the world, in all types of businesses, rely on computers to communicate through e-mail and

Computers are almost everywhere and can be an excellent, and essential, learning resource. Training in how to use the latest technology could be one of the smartest moves you'll ever make.

When you have a cell phone, you can make important connections from just about any location.

cell phones include the ability to connect to the Internet, send messages and take photographs, and make video recordings.

To use this technology, you need a cell phone and a plan purchased from a service provider. You can obtain plans where you buy a certain number of minutes. Another option is to pay a monthly charge that covers a set number of minutes. If you go over that time, you pay a fee.

Learning Through Technology

Technology doesn't just make doing your job easier; it also makes learning more convenient. Because you live in a high-tech age, you no longer have to rely only on books and taking courses in the traditional way, whereby a teacher lectures in a classroom setting. Thanks to information technology, people are able to earn a degree, learn new skills, and conduct research from almost anywhere, on their own schedule, and, to some degree, at their own pace.

You can search for information or look for a job on a computer using the Internet.

The Internet

The Internet is an excellent resource for gaining knowledge. As you know, when you conduct research, you want to use many sources. The Internet works in much the same way, only you don't have to run around looking for information. The sources are more or less in one place.

The Internet is a worldwide collection of networks, which are groups of computers talking to each other. Millions of computer networks join together and agree to share information. People connect to the Internet through a service provider. This is a business that uses powerful technology to offer connections to the Internet in a way that individual computers, or even small networks, couldn't accomplish on their own.

Using the Internet for learning means that you have access to many sources of knowledge right at your fingertips. You can find information on the Internet in a number of ways. There are informal, self-directed searches, where you can find information on your own, and more formal online learning offered by universities and educational organizations.

Self-Directed Searches

No one person, organization, or service provider owns the Internet. Almost anyone can share information. One way this universal sharing is done is through Web sites, which are electronic pages of images and words. The information on these pages is the content.

You can learn a great deal by looking at various Web sites. The people and groups who make these pages available on the Internet (a practice called posting) are eager to share what they know. Therefore, Web sites generally contain plenty of information.

Finding Web Sites by Using Search Engines

You can usually track down what you need by using a search engine. Two popular search engines that you might have heard of are Yahoo! and Google. To use a search engine, type in a word or string of words that

Check Your Sources

Nearly anyone, not just experts on certain topics, can post information on the Internet. Not every piece of information that you find on the Web is reliable. So, how can you be reasonably sure that the information you have obtained is correct? Consider the source of the information.

For example, if you want to find out about your favorite television show, you would go to the show's official TV network Web site. What you read there is probably the most accurate and complete information about the program because the people who post that information work on or for the show. They are experts on that subject. Fans can post information about the TV show, but they are not directly involved in the making of the program and, consequently, they don't know all the facts about it.

Likewise, the information you are seeking about a company is bound to be more up-to-date and accurate if you find the information on the company's own Web site, rather than on a site created by someone who isn't connected to the company.

concern the subject you are investigating. The search engine will then find where those words appear on all the Web sites on the Internet. Be as specific as you can when you are typing in search words.

Job-Related Internet Searches

When it comes to finding a job, you can—and should—investigate Web sites that have information on job openings, job search techniques, and career planning, to name a few topics. Also, more and more companies prefer to receive applications and resumes over the Internet, so you should learn how to post your materials online. Many places have instructions that walk you through each step for online submissions.

Search for Web sites that offer information on companies where you might want to work, including stories about the bosses who run those businesses. Learning about the company and the people who work there gives you a better idea of whether or not your skills match those they are looking for, and if you'd enjoy working there.

Searches can also help you learn new skills that can make a job you already have more rewarding. For example, you might find a better way to perform a task or overcome a work problem by reading about it on the Web site of a group that has faced a similar situation.

Interactive Technology

Learning online doesn't have to be limited to your finding written information and not being able to ask questions or get feedback on that information. You can also have "conversations" online by using interactive technology. This is a great way to build a network of people in your line of work, and you can use these contacts as a source of information. Two forms of interactive technology that would be helpful to look into are:

- **Blogs.** The word "blog" is a short form of "Web log." These Web sites contain text, images, and links that focus on a certain subject. They are posted in chronological order (by date) and written in a

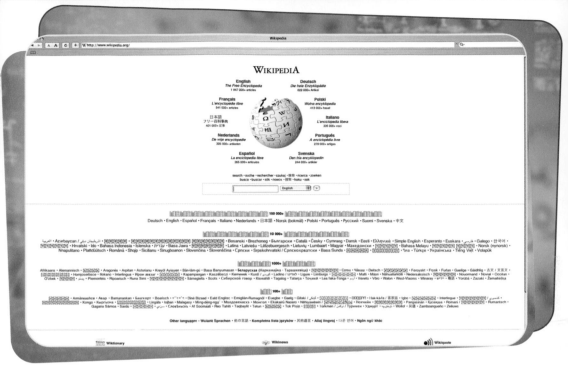

The "online encyclopedia" Wikipedia (http://wikipedia.org) is not just an electronic source of information. It can also be considered a social network because many people often come together to create one entry.

personal and informal style, similar to a journal. Blogs usually contain space for readers to post comments and chat with the person who posted the blog and other readers.

- **Wikis.** A wiki is a Web site on a certain topic that lets people add information to, or delete information from, items already posted online. Whole groups of people can contribute to the making of one wiki entry. It's interesting to read the opinions and knowledge of so many people and to add your own thoughts. Still, the fact that anyone can post makes some people think wikis don't always give reliable information. The most well-known wiki is Wikipedia (http://wikipedia.org), which calls itself an online encyclopedia.

Distance or Online Learning

A more formal way to become further educated by using the Internet is to sign up for an online learning program. Also known as distance learning, online learning is when you participate in classes from your home or another location, not in a school building or classroom. Lessons are available online. You complete assignments on your own, returning your work through e-mail or some other computer program designed specifically for this purpose.

Many colleges, and even some high schools and middle schools, offer online learning courses. Some businesses also provide online courses, including seminars that might take only a week or a day to complete. A variety of subjects are offered online. Students can either learn a trade, such as plumbing, or take classes that will count toward earning a certificate or a degree from a university. Moreover, getting an education by using the Internet makes it easier for those people who hold down a full-time job to continue their learning while they work.

Technical Training

Suppose what you need to learn is how to use technology itself. If you don't feel very confident about using technology, don't worry. There are plenty of places where you

Distance learning may include watching taped lessons on cable television, as well as working on assignments through your computer.

can get training in high-tech equipment and processes. Colleges and junior colleges, local community programs, and private businesses all offer training in using the latest technology.

Some company Web sites have online tutorials, or lessons, on how to use their product or perform a task. Tutorials usually guide you step-by-step and let you practice your skills, so you don't have to have a lot of technical knowledge to operate them. This kind of online learning is helpful if you need to learn skills fast and don't have time for more formal training.

chapter four

REFLECT AND EVALUATE

The world of work is full of change. New technology and customer demands mean workers cannot rely on one set of skills or a single way of thinking for long. Past accomplishments are quickly forgotten as fresh challenges rise up every day. The hard truth is that at work—as in life—people tend to think you're only as good as what you've done lately. You have to keep using, practicing, and updating your skills and learning to keep up with the competition.

Imagine that someone has taught you a lesson, but then you quickly forget it and go back to an old way of doing things. Maybe the person who is teaching you gets frustrated, and he or she says, "Haven't you learned this by now?" The truth is, in this situation, you haven't learned. Sure, you might have understood the lesson at first, but when the time came, you didn't put it into practice. True learning involves retention, meaning that you remember and practice what you have learned, as well as a willingness and the ability to use that knowledge whenever it is appropriate.

Learning isn't valuable when it's only temporary. To make lessons stick, you need to reflect on what you've learned and evaluate how well you've learned it.

Reflection

Reflection is thinking, but in a way that goes beyond what you might normally do when you're making a quick decision or trying to remember facts. You need to break down a subject into chunks you can manage and ask yourself a lot of questions about each chunk when you reflect on something. In other words, reflection is thinking with purpose, and the purpose is learning.

Analyzing, or examining closely, your past learning experiences one piece at a time is a good start. Review what has gone right and any trouble areas you may have come across. Then think deeply not just about the decisions you have made but also the reasons why you made those particular decisions. Look at how things turned out when you made each learning choice and what effect your actions had on the results. Remember to be honest with yourself, and don't shy away from the stuff that doesn't make you look so good. You can learn from your mistakes as well as your successes.

Reflection is a useful learning tool because it helps you avoid mistakes you may have made in the past. The idea is to pay careful attention to what has happened so that you can make even better moves in the future. This takes time. Don't try to rush through reflection.

Critical Thinking

Reflection and evaluation are examples of what's known as critical thinking. This is thinking with a specific goal in mind: to make a situation better.

Critical thinking is different from rote learning, which is simply memorizing something and then repeating or acting on it without fully understanding it or caring. Critical thinking means you are aware of the value of what you are learning and you put it to good use. When you are aware, you consider all the possibilities. When you do that, you come up with better solutions to problems, and there is less of a chance that you will make a mistake. Critical thinking involves the following:

- Asking questions in order to solve problems
- Researching and gathering information that helps answer the questions you have asked
- Finding solutions that make the most sense out of all possible solutions
- Testing solutions in real-life situations
- Accepting that your solutions may not work out and being willing to begin the critical-thinking process all over again

Research and gathering information are vital critical-thinking skills.

Evaluation

Along with reflection comes evaluation. When you evaluate, you decide whether or not an idea is worth having or an event is worth experiencing. Evaluating your ability to learn would require figuring out how much you have learned and how valuable that learning is to your future success.

Generally, you do this by comparing your level of knowledge to that of other people in a similar situation, or to what the requirements are for a particular job. For instance, if you were looking for a job as an executive assistant, you would be expected to have excellent computer skills and be able to pull together lengthy reports quickly. You can evaluate whether you have these skills by measuring how fast you can type (or, in computer language, keyboard) and how quickly you compile accurate information while researching and writing a paper for school.

You can also evaluate your success on a personal level. Before you began your learning experience, you listed goals that you wanted to reach. Evaluating whether or not you met your goals is a worthwhile activity.

To evaluate, you need to be objective. That means you shouldn't let your emotions get in the way of your thinking. You need to think clearly and calmly when you reflect, paying attention to the facts surrounding your learning experiences. Judging yourself also requires balance. You don't want to be too hard on yourself, but you don't want to let yourself off the hook either.

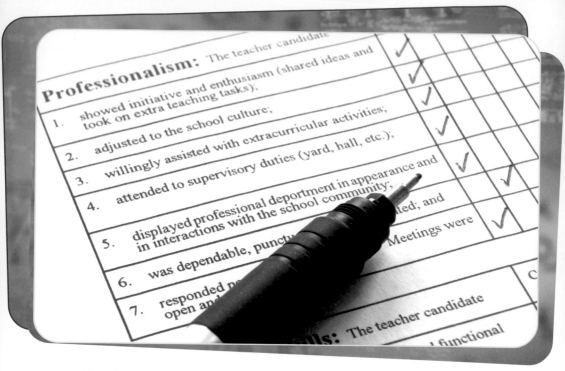

Professionalism: The teacher candidate

1. showed initiative and enthusiasm (shared ideas and took on extra teaching tasks);

2. adjusted to the school culture;

3. willingly assisted with extracurricular activities;

4. attended to supervisory duties (yard, hall, etc.);

5. displayed professional deportment in appearance and in interactions with the school community;

6. was dependable, punct... ...ted; and

7. responded ... open an...

Meetings were

...ls: The teacher candidate

...functional

Grading yourself on your skill level and how well you've performed specific tasks is a type of evaluation.

Evaluation comes into play in the workplace all the time. Bosses and coworkers evaluate how well you handle individual projects, manage your time, meet deadlines, and work as part of a team. Then, each year, your total work performance is evaluated to see if you should get a raise and, if so, how large it should be. If you have a poor evaluation at any time, you may be put on probation or even fired. Self-evaluation lets you take steps to improve any trouble spots before someone in authority has a chance to threaten your employment.

Questions for Self-Evaluation

After you have learned a new skill and have moved on to the evaluation stage, you'll want to ask yourself some hard questions. Here are some questions that might help you with self-evaluation, as suggested by the Study Guides and Strategies Web site author Joe Landsberger:

1) What did I do right?
2) What could I do better?
3) Did my plan take into account my strengths and weaknesses?
4) Did I choose the right conditions?
5) Did I follow through, and was I disciplined with myself?
6) Did I succeed?
7) Have I taken time to celebrate my success?

Outcomes

Reflection and evaluation are necessary to determine whether or not you have met the goals you set for yourself when you started a learning experience. This involves learning outcomes, which demonstrates that you have gained the knowledge and skills you set out to get. Put simply, learning outcomes show what you can do with what you have learned.

Outcomes benefit you, the worker, as well as future employers. They give you a target to aim for by clearly defining your goals and what it will take to meet those goals. You'll be able to tell right away if you have successfully learned something when you

Getting feedback is one of the best ways to find out whether or not you have met your learning goals.

are able to put that knowledge into action in a very concrete way.

Be as specific as possible when you decide how to describe outcomes. If they are too general, such as "Improve computer skills," then it will be harder for you or anyone else to figure out if you have reached that goal. More specifically, make the outcome something like "Learn how to use PowerPoint so I can create a presentation on monthly expenses at the next staff meeting."

Get Feedback

You can best tell if your outcomes are on target if you share what you have learned. See what others have to say about your conclusions. They can either confirm that you've come to a correct conclusion, or help you see different answers you hadn't considered before. This is called getting feedback, and it's an important step in evaluating your progress. Education experts have shown that sharing ideas makes it more likely that you will enjoy the learning process and, therefore, stick with it.

You can get feedback from either one individual or a group, in person or at a distance (on the phone or by e-mail). In school, you receive feedback from your teacher and classmates. In the workplace, you get feedback from your boss and coworkers after you give a presentation or write a report. This also happens when you discuss a problem during a meeting or suggest a product or service to a client.

Where You Are Now

Once you have reflected on and evaluated your outcomes and have gotten feedback, you should take a look at where you stand one more time. It will not be in the same place you were before you began your learning experience. Is it where you expected to be? Hopefully. But even if it is not, you can still make the most of what you have learned.

Perhaps your learning experience didn't help you arrive at the specific goal you were aiming for, but you

When you make the commitment to learn throughout your life, you'll be looking at a strong and bright future.

did learn something along the way. You may be able to adapt these new skills to fit your need. Or, believe it or not, your reflection may lead you to change your goal to something totally different. Another option is to simply save what you have learned for another time. You never know when a skill might come in handy.

The point is that nothing you learn is ever wasted. Corny as it may sound, learning how to learn is itself a great achievement. It prepares you for the future because now you know how the process works. The next time you need to learn new skills for work—and the way the job market keeps changing, there will be a next time— you'll already be a step ahead.

Consequently, you have every reason to be happy with your efforts. Be proud of your new skills, and take a couple of minutes to simply celebrate the fact that you are now a lifelong learner. You've earned it.

glossary

auditory Having to do with hearing.

conclusion A decision you come to after research and thinking.

experiential learning Learning by hands-on, real-life experience.

expertise An area in which a person is an expert.

hypothesis What you suppose will happen based on the facts in front of you.

interpersonal Between people.

posting Putting text and images (pictures and graphics) on a Web site.

probation A trial period in which a person's fitness for a job is tested.

recommendation When someone tells an employer, usually in a letter, the reasons why he or she would be a good employee.

retain To keep or remember.

socialize To be friendly and work or play with others.

stipend A small amount of money paid to workers such as apprentices and interns; similar to an allowance.

tactile Having to do with touch.

truant Being away from school without permission.

tutorial Special instruction.

visual Having to do with sight.

vocational Having to do with someone's job or career; work-related.

Council for Adult and Experiential Learning
55 East Monroe Street, Suite 1930
Chicago, IL 60603
(312) 499-2600
Web site: http://www.cael.org
The council provides access to education through partner-
    ships with business, government, labor, and higher
    education. CAEL offers adult learner services such
    as workplace training and workforce development.

Jobs for the Future
88 Broad Street
Boston, MA 02110
(617) 728-4446
Web site: http://www.jff.org
Jobs for the Future helps lifelong learners get the edu-
    cation they need to advance on the job. Particular
    focus areas include skills training, workforce
    development, and literacy.

Service Canada
Citizen and Community Service General Inquiries
140 Promenade du Portage
Place du Portage, Phase IV, 4th Floor
Gatineau, QC K1A 0J9
Canada
(800) 277-9914
Web site: http://www.servicecanada.gc.ca
This Canadian agency provides information about
    career opportunities, career planning, and resume
    writing and job interviewing techniques.

U.S. Office of Vocational and Adult Education
U.S. Department of Education
Office of Vocational and Adult Education
400 Maryland Avenue SW
Washington, DC 20202-7100
(202) 245-7700
Web site: http://www.ed.gov/about/offices/list/ovae/
index.html?src = mr
The OVAE Web site has information that will help prepare
young people and adults for postsecondary education, successful careers, and productive lives. Links
include the Work-Based Learning Project, which is
designed to provide best practices, tools, tips, and
learning communities. In English and Spanish.

Web Sites

Due to the changing nature of Internet links, Rosen
Publishing has developed an online list of Web sites
related to the subject of this book. This site is updated
regularly. Please use this link to access the list:

http://www.rosenlinks.com/wr/llsk

for further reading

Bachel, Beverly K. *What Do You Really Want? How to Set a Goal and Go for It! A Guide for Teens.* Minneapolis, MN: Free Spirit Publishing, 2001.

Bilwas, Ron. *The C Student's Guide to Success: How to Become a High Achiever Without the Best Grades, Connections, or Pedigrǣ.* New York, NY: Penguin Group, 2007.

Bolles, Richard Nelson. *What Color Is Your Parachute for Teens.* Berkeley, CA: Ten Speed Press, 2006.

Fireside, Bryna J. *Choices for the High School Graduate: A Survival Guide for the Information Age.* New York, NY: Ferguson Publishing Co., 2000.

Greene, Rebecca, and Elizabeth Verdick. *The Teenagers' Guide to School Outside the Box.* Minneapolis, MN: Free Spirit Publishing, 2001.

Ireland, Susan. *Complete Idiot's Guide to Cool Jobs for Teens.* Indianapolis, IN: Alpha Books, 2001.

Marks-Beale, Abby. *Success Skills: Strategies for Study and Lifelong Learning.* Belmont, CA: South-Western Educational Publishing (Thompson), 2006.

Schwager, Tina, and Michele Schuerger. *Cool Women, Hot Jobs: And How You Can Go for It, Too!* Minneapolis, MN: Free Spirit Publishing, 2002.

Whitaker, Urban. *Career Success: A Step-by-Step Workbook for Students, Job Seekers and Lifelong Learners.* Oakland, CA: O'Brien and Whitaker, 2002.

Zielin, Laura. *Make Things Happen: The Key to Networking for Teens.* Montreal, Quebec: Lobster Prcss, 2003.

bibliography

Acharya, Chandrama. "Employers' Feedback: A Source of Information on Students' Learning Outcome." Retrieved June 23, 2007 (http://www.cdtl.nus.edu.sg/link/Mar2002/feedback2.htm).

Allen, I. Eileen, and Jeff Seaman. *Growing by Degrees: Online Education in the United States, 2005.* Wellesley, MA: Sloan Consortium, 2005.

Association for Career and Technical Education. "What's Career Tech? Frequently Asked Questions." Retrieved June 16, 2007 (http://www.acteonline.org/career_tech/faq.cfm).

Cunningham, Ward, and Bo Leuf. "What Is Wiki?" June 27, 2002 (http://wiki.org/wiki.cgi?WhatIsWiki).

EFF Center for Training and Technical Assistance, Center for Literacy Studies, University of Tennessee. "Equipped for the Future." Retrieved March 30, 2007 (http://eff.cls.utk.edu/toolkit/standards_wheel.htm).

Gay, Greg (adapted by J. Ivanco). "Multiple Intelligences Inventory." Retrieved June 19, 2007 (http://www.ldrc.ca/projects/miinventory/mitest.html).

Gross, Ron. "How to Be a Better Lifelong Learner." Retrieved June 15, 2007 (http://adulted.about.com/cs/selfstudy/a/socrates_advice.htm).

Gross, Ron. *Socrates Way: Seven Master Keys to Using Your Mind to the Utmost.* New York, NY: Putnam, 2002.

Hotta Dover, Kimeiko. "Self-Directed Learning." Retrieved June 17, 2007 (http://adulted.about.com/cs/selfstudy/a/self_study_plan.htm).

Landsberger, Joe. "Study Guides and Strategies." Retrieved June 17, 2007 (http://www.studygs.net/metacognition.htm).

LdPride.net. "Learning Styles Explained." Retrieved June 20, 2007 (http://www.ldpride.net/learningstyles. MI.htm#What%20are).

Marshall, Brian. "How Wikis Work." July 13, 2005. Retrieved June 16, 2007 (http://computer. howstuffworks.com/wiki.htm).

McMaster University, Center for Student Development. "Learning Styles and Learning Style Assessments." Retrieved June 2007 (http://csd.mcmaster.ca/ academic/learning_styles.htm).

Open Learn Learning Space. "Defining Reflection." May 29, 2007. Retrieved June 20, 2007 (http://openlearn. open.ac.uk/mod/resource/view.php?id=160191).

Paul, Richard. "Critical Thinking: Basic Questions and Answers." 2004. Retrieved June 23, 2007 (http://www.criticalthinking.org/aboutCT/ CTquestionsAnswers.shtml).

Paul, Richard. *Critical Thinking: How to Prepare Students for a Rapidly Changing World*. Dillon Beach, CA: Foundation for Critical Thinking, 1995.

Rama, Dasaratha V. "Service-Learning Outcomes, Reflection and Assessment." August 2001. Retrieved June 23, 2007 (http://www.compact.org/disciplines/ reflection/outcomes).

The Sloan Consortium. "Growing by Degrees: Online Education in the United States, 2005." November 2005. Retrieved June 16, 2007 (http://www. sloanc.org/publications/survey/pdf/growing_by_ degrees.pdf).

St. Amand, David. "Self-Directed Learning." Retrieved June 20, 2007 (http://adulted.about.com/cs/

selfstudy/a/SDL_arcand.htm?terms = continuing +
education + credit).

Teaching Support Services. "Learning Objectives: A Basic
Guide." Fall 2003. Retrieved June 23, 2007 (http://
liad.gbrownc.on.ca/programs/InsAdult/currlo.htm).

Tyson, Jeff. "How Internet Infrastructure Works." April 3,
2001. Retrieved June 16, 2007 (http://computer.
howstuffworks.com/internet-infrastructure.htm).

Virginia Employment Commission. "The Mid-Atlantic
Guide to Information on Careers (MAGIC)." June
2002. Retrieved June 2007 (http://www.vec.state.
va.us/pdf/lmi_magic.pdf).

Wilson, Cynthia, et al. "Defining and Teaching Learning
Outcomes." June 24, 2001. Retrieved June 23, 2007
(http://www.league.org/league/projects/lcp/lcp3/
Learning_Outcomes.htm).

World Bank Group. "Lifelong Learning." 2001. Retrieved
June 16, 2007 (http://www1.worldbank.org/
education/lifelong_learning/overview.asp).

index

About the Author

Jeanne Nagle is a writer and editor at the Rochester Institute of Technology in upstate New York. Her experiences at RIT and elsewhere in higher education have given her keen insight into the methods and benefits of lifelong learning.

Photo Credits

Cover (top, left to right) www.istockphoto.com/Lise Gagne, © www.istockphoto.com/dagmar heymans, © www.istockphoto.com/ jim pruitt; cover (middle, left to right) © www.istockphoto.com/ anne stahl, © www.istockphoto.com/Joan Kimball; cover (bottom, left to right) © www.istockphoto.com/Willie B. Thomas, © www.istockphoto.com/Chris Schmidt, © www.istockphoto.com/ Sandra O'Claire; pp. 6, 20, 34, 46 (left to right) © www.istockphoto. com/Sandra O'Claire, © www.istockphoto.com/Chris Schmidt, © www.istockphoto.com/Andrey Popov; p. 7 © Rod Morata/Stone/ Getty Images; p. 9 © www.istockphoto.com/Livingimages; p. 10 © www.istockphoto.com/Linda & Colin McKie; p. 12 © John Birdsall/The Image Works; p. 15 © age footstock/SuperStock; p. 18 © www.istockphoto.com/Andrei Tchernov; p. 21 © www. istockphoto.com/Laurence Gough; p. 22 © Mike Greenlar/The Image Works; p. 27 © Bob Daemmrich/The Image Works; p. 29 © www.istockphoto.com/Jamie Wilson; p. 32 © Tim Boyle/Getty Images; p. 35 © www.istockphoto.com/dpms; p. 37 © www. istockphoto.com/Stefan Klein; p. 38 © www.istockphoto.com/ Nicole S. Young; pp. 39, 49 Shutterstock.com; p. 45 © Najiah Feanny/Corbis; p. 50 © www.istockphoto.com/Cindy England; p. 52 © www.istockphoto.com/Tomaz Levstek; p. 54 © www. istockphoto.com/Sheryl Griffin.

Designer: Nelson Sá; **Editor:** Kathy Campbell
Photo Researcher: Amy Feinberg